A Note From Denise Renner

The Word of God is so powerful in our lives. It is essential that every person spend time with God and study His Word in order to stay spiritually strong in these last days.

This study guide corresponds to my *TIME With Denise Renner* TV program by the same title that can be viewed at **deniserenner.org**. My desire is that through these lessons, you find the encouragement and freedom in Christ that you need. I believe the Holy Spirit is going to speak to you through the words you read in this study tool and that as you begin to use it, you will be *propelled* into the abundant life God has planned for you. I encourage you to make the effort to receive all He has for you and all He wants to do in you — it will definitely be worth it!

Whether you have walked with the Lord a long time or have just begun to follow Him, there is so much He wants to give you from His Word. He sees where you are, and He wants to meet you there.

> **Therefore do not worry about tomorrow, for tomorrow**
> **will worry about its own things.**
> **Sufficient for the day is its own trouble.**
> **— Matthew 6:34**

Your sister and friend in Jesus Christ,

Denise Renner

Denise Renner

Who You Are Called To Be

Copyright © 2024 by Denise Renner
1814 W. Tacoma St.
Broken Arrow, OK 74012-1406

Published by Rick Renner Ministries
www.renner.org

ISBN 13: 978-1-6675-0964-8

eBook ISBN 13: 978-1-6675-0965-5

TOPIC

Who We Are

SCRIPTURES

1. **James 1:18** — Of His own will He brought us forth by the word of truth, that we might be a kind of firstfruits of His creatures.

2. **Psalm 139:13-16** — For You formed my inward parts; You covered me in my mother's womb. I will praise You, for I am fearfully and wonderfully made; marvelous are Your works, and that my soul knows very well. My frame was not hidden from You, when I was made in secret, and skillfully wrought in the lowest parts of the earth. Your eyes saw my substance, being yet unformed. And in Your book they all were written, the days fashioned for me, when as yet there were none of them.

3. **James 1:1** — James, a bondservant of God and of the Lord Jesus Christ, to the twelve tribes which are scattered abroad: Greetings.

4. **Philippians 1:6** — . . . being confident of this very thing, that He who has begun a good work in you will complete it until the day of Jesus Christ.

5. **Hebrews 12:2** — . . . looking unto Jesus, the author and finisher of our faith, who for the joy that was set before Him endured the cross, despising the shame, and has sat down at the right hand of the throne of God.

6. **Hebrews 12:11** — Now no chastening seems to be joyful for the present, but painful; nevertheless, afterward it yields the peaceable fruit of righteousness to those who have been trained by it.

SYNOPSIS

The five lessons in this study on *Who You Are Called To Be* will focus on the following topics:

- Who We Are
- There Is Something You Must Hear
- Your Words Are Powerful

- Bitterness Never Looks Good on You
- Don't Forget What You Saw in the Mirror

The Bible says that if you are a born-again child of God, the same Spirit that raised Jesus Christ from the dead lives in you! (*See* Romans 8:11.) This Spirit is the Holy Spirit of God Himself, and He is an unstoppable force. As you begin to get a revelation of the powerhouse Person living in you and who you are in Christ, you, too, become unstoppable.

The emphasis of this lesson:

You were saved and brought forth into Christ, not by your own will, but by the will of God Himself, because your life has great purpose. Everything that makes you uniquely you was designed by God to enable you to fulfill His specific assignment for your life.

Redemption and Salvation Are God's Idea — Not Ours

The first step to really knowing who you are in Christ and understanding His purpose for your life is realizing that your salvation was God's idea — not yours. Jesus plainly stated, "You did not choose Me, but I chose you and appointed you that you should go and bear fruit, and that your fruit should remain..." (John 15:16). This truth is also talked about by James in his letter to the believers in Christ that had been scattered across the Roman Empire. He said:

> **Of His own will He brought us forth by the word of truth, that we might be a kind of firstfruits of His creatures.**
> **— James 1:18**

This was a very strong and significant statement coming from James. History tells us that he was the half-brother of Jesus, and during the years of Jesus' ministry, James did not believe in Jesus. As a matter of fact, James was so resistant to the Lord that he was a vocal adversary of Jesus' ministry. After Jesus died and came back to life, James repented of his sins, surrendered his life to God, and became a powerful leader in the Early Church.

It was this same James who said, "Of His own will He brought us forth by the word of truth..." (James 1:18). If you take a moment and personalize this verse, you could insert yourself in it and say:

> Of His own will He brought *ME* forth by the word of truth, that *I* might be a kind of firstfruits of His creatures.

From the foundation of the world, it was God's desire to birth you — yes *YOU* — into His family through your faith in Jesus Christ. His presence in your life enables you to walk in victory and be unstoppable. Regardless of what you are experiencing right now, know that God has designed a place that is tailormade just for you. You were birthed on the earth for such a time as this to fulfill a *specific* destiny! (*See* Esther 4:14.)

You Are One of a Kind!

Many people are simply fascinated by all the different types of cars that have been manufactured over the years. From Rolls Royce and Mercedes models to Ferraris and Lamborghinis, these high-performance and luxurious vehicles are highly sought after and extremely costly in value. With each one, an instruction manual is available that details every single part and mechanism that makes it run and work the way it does.

In the same way, God has intricately designed each of us in very unique ways. David was so awestruck by the Lord's work, he said:

> For You formed my inward parts; You covered me in my mother's womb. I will praise You, for I am fearfully and wonderfully made; marvelous are Your works, and that my soul knows very well. My frame was not hidden from You, when I was made in secret, and skillfully wrought in the lowest parts of the earth. Your eyes saw my substance, being yet unformed. And in Your book they all were written, the days fashioned for me, when as yet there were none of them.
> — Psalm 139:13-16

Think about it. When you were inside your mother's womb, all the intricate parts that make you "you" were being formed and put into place. Along with the color of your hair, eyes, and skin, your exact height, facial features, and even your foot and hand size were all determined and pro-grammed into your DNA. Furthermore, every day of your life was written down in His book *before* any of those days took place. Every function and facet was wired into you by God Himself, and you are way more valuable than a car or any piece of machinery known to man.

Things made by human hands may be valuable, but they don't come close to your worth. Things are temporary, but your life is eternal. You were made to live forever in relationship with God.

What Made James' Message So Powerful?

When James wrote his New Testament letter, he was writing to First-Century believers who were suffering persecution for their faith in Jesus. He opened by saying:

> **James, a bondservant of God and of the Lord Jesus Christ, to the twelve tribes which are scattered abroad: Greetings.**
> **— James 1:1**

Interestingly, in the original Greek text, this verse actually says:

> **James, a bondservant of God WHO IS the Lord Jesus Christ, to the twelve tribes which are scattered abroad.**
> **— James 1:1**

Essentially, James was declaring, "Jesus Christ *is God.*" Imagine that! Jesus, whom James had repeatedly denied while He was alive, was now being proclaimed by James to be *God.*

By the time James wrote his letter, God had drastically transformed his life into that of a humble servant. Historians tell us that he became the pastor of the church in Jerusalem, and he was on his knees in prayer so often and for so long that he developed thick callouses, giving him knees that resembled a camel. Hence, his nickname was "Old Camel Knees."

James wanted his persecuted brothers and sisters to know that they were saved and brought forth into Christ by the will of God Himself and not their own will. In the same way, you, too, were born again because it was God's will. He is the One who put faith in your heart to believe in and receive Jesus as your Savior and Lord (*see* Ephesians 2:8,9).

Everyone's Life Has a Purpose

The Bible says, "God made everything with a place and *purpose…*" (Proverbs 16:4 *MSG*). Therefore, your life is not a meaningless existence, and you are not a mistake. You have a purpose — a major assignment with multiple minor assignments all along the way.

Everything about you — your physical characteristics, your mannerisms, the way you think, your personality, your weaknesses and strengths, and even your life's experiences — all make you uniquely you and enable you to fulfill God's assignment for your life. Again, you have a purpose, and nothing about you is an accident or by coincidence. You are perfectly designed to carry out God's plan for your life.

Just as windmills are designed with huge, broad blades to catch the wind and effortlessly function to create energy, your life is uniquely designed to catch the "wind" of the Holy Spirit and function for God's glory. Rather than making you work yourself silly trying to force something to happen in your own strength, the Lord wants you to rest in Him and allow His wind to blow through your life, functioning in the design with which He created you.

Jesus said, "...Come to me. Get away with me and you'll recover your life. I'll show you how to take a real rest. Walk with me and work with me — watch how I do it. Learn the unforced rhythms of grace. I won't lay anything heavy or ill-fitting on you. Keep company with me and you'll learn to live freely and lightly" (Matthew 11:28-30 *MSG*).

Each of us is like an instrument or tool in God's toolbox. Some of us are hammers, some are screwdrivers, others are wrenches, and still others are tape measures. If you are a screwdriver trying to do the job of a hammer, you are going to beat yourself silly and not accomplish very much. We each need to stay in our lane, work in our wheelhouse, and function in the way God designed us.

God Called You To Be *YOU*!

One of the most damaging things we can do is compare ourselves with others. Inevitably, this will either puff us up in pride or leave us feeling inept and insecure because others seem to be so much better at certain things than we are. Denise candidly shared this story from her own life regarding the danger of comparison:

> Many years ago, when my husband Rick and I were traveling in ministry, we would often visit a particular church that was on fire for God. The pastor, his wife, and their family were wonderful. The pastor's wife was very domesticated and could do just about anything. She had a vibrant garden, made beautiful rugs, and educated her children.

I couldn't do any of those things. At that time, it took all my energy and efforts just to accompany Rick as he traveled around teaching the Word. I was constantly called upon to meet and greet total strangers and connect with them on a personal level, all the while trying to look presentable. Likewise, it was my job to stand in front of people and minister in song, hoping and praying for God's anointing to show up and flow through me.

Unfortunately, every time we went to that church, I would fall into the trap of comparing myself with the pastor's wife, and I never seemed to measure up. Sadly, I came to a place where I began to say to myself, *I'm just not enough. I need to be more like her. But because I can't be more like her, I'm just going to pull back, be quiet, and hide myself.* And that's what I did for years. The result of all my comparing was that it shut down all my giftings and freedom and short circuited the way God made me.

To be clear, that pastor's wife was a wonderful woman who didn't do anything wrong. The problem was with *me*. God didn't call me to be her or my husband Rick or anyone else. He called me to be ME. Likewise, *God called you to be you* — not your sister, your brother, or your best friend. It's your job to learn what your calling is and cooperate with God to be the best you that you can be.

Friend, don't compare or compete; it will only leave you in defeat. And don't apologize for your personality or for the way you look physically. God Himself, according to His will, birthed you into the world right now to fulfill His purpose. He is the One who gave life to the specific egg and sperm that united in your mother's womb. He put His breath in your lungs and continues to cause your heart to beat. You are fearfully and wonderfully made in the image of God, perfectly prepared to fulfill His purpose for your life.

Our Experiences Are Vital and Valuable in God's Hands

Each of our lives is a visible display of God's mercy and grace, and Heather Z's story is a perfect example. From the age of seven until her senior year in high school, Heather was actively involved in gymnastics. At the age of 12, she was involved in an accident that literally broke her neck. It was a C1 break, which greatly affects the lungs and one's ability to breathe. It's considered "hangman's vertebra" because when a person hangs himself, C1 is what breaks, cutting off all air flow and causing him or her to suffocate to death.

In Heather's case, she was rushed to the hospital, and after numerous preliminary tests were conducted, she was wheeled down to the X-ray room and positioned on a table for a series of images to be taken. It was there on that table that Heather died and went to Heaven.

While she was there, she saw several people who she knew had already passed away, but most importantly, she came face to face with the very presence of God. It happened that as she was looking up into the sky, she saw what looked like two huge hands that began to fill the heavens. Suddenly, those hands swooped down and cupped together under her, lifting her up in great strength.

"I then heard a voice begin to speak to me," Heather said. "And it was the voice of the Lord. We communicated with each other spirit to spirit, and I remember that as the Lord spoke to me, He told me things about my life. What I will never forget is when He said, 'Heather, there's going to be a time in the future when I'm going to come to you and remind you of this experience, and you're going to need it. But don't worry; everything is going to be okay. I have you in the palm of My hands, and I have many more assignments for you.'"

Miraculously, God brought Heather's dead body back to life and fused the broken bones in her neck! Her life still had much purpose. Not everyone is given the opportunity to die, be swept up into God's presence, and hear His voice. He needed her to continue to function and flow in the power of His Spirit to accomplish His plans.

And just as Heather's experiences and gifts are valuable, so are yours. What you have gone through is vital and valuable in God's hands. As you cooperate with Him, He will take the messes you've experienced and make them a message that brings Him glory.

God Is With You!

Writing under the inspiration of the Holy Spirit, the apostle Paul declared this very powerful promise to us from the Father in Philippians 1:6.

Being confident of this very thing, that He who has begun a good work in you will complete it until the day of Jesus Christ.

What God started in you, He will finish! The healing, the restoration, and the renewing of your mind that He began, He intends to complete. It is His lifelong commitment to you. Your part is to listen for the voice of His Spirit and obediently cooperate with His directions.

Remember, God is the Author and Finisher of your faith (*see* Hebrews 12:2). If you are saved, He has already authored — or started — your faith by birthing you into His family through Jesus. So right now, you are somewhere in between the beginning and the end, and right there with you in the middle is the Lord Himself! He's running the race with you, giving you His life's strength to make it through each day until He finishes what He started.

Friend, God is Faithful! He has brought you through many things in the past that you thought you wouldn't survive — but you did because of Him! Feed your soul on His faithfulness. Grab hold of those past experiences and deliberately choose to anchor your faith in Him. Tell yourself, *What God did before, He will do again. His power has not diminished. He is still well able to strengthen me and deliver me through this situation.*

"Jesus Christ is the same yesterday, today, and forever" (Hebrews 13:8). He pulled you out before, and He will pull you out again. No matter what you're going through right now, know that in this moment, God is with you — and He will not leave you. The writer of Hebrews confirms this, telling us:

> …[God] Himself has said, I will not in any way fail you nor give you up nor leave you without support. [I will] not, [I will] not, [I will] not in any degree leave you helpless nor forsake nor let [you] down (relax My hold on you)! [Assuredly not!]
> — Hebrews 13:5 (*AMPC*)

May the Lord open your spiritual eyes to see His presence active in your life right now. May His Spirit of truth give you a heart-revelation of your calling and purpose and a realization of just how precious you are to the Father. He loves you. You didn't choose Him — He has chosen you and designed everything about you for such a time as this. May you cease all self-doubt and striving to make things happen in your own strength and allow the peace and love of God to flood your soul.

STUDY QUESTIONS

Be diligent to present yourself approved to God, a worker
who does not need to be ashamed, rightly dividing the word of truth.
— 2 Timothy 2:15

1. What new insights did you learn about the half-brother of Jesus
    named James, who wrote the New Testament book of James?

2. God chose *you* to be His child. It was "of His will" — not your own.
    Take time to reflect on Isaiah 49:1 and 2; Jeremiah 1:5; Acts 17:26,
    and Ephesians 1:4. Write down what the Lord shows you about being
    handpicked by Him.

3. One of the most damaging things we can do is compare ourselves with
    others. What does the Bible have to say in Second Corinthians 10:12
    about the dangers of comparison?

4. Take a few moments to read through Psalm 139 — paying special
    attention to verses 1-4 and 13-18. What is the Holy Spirit showing
    you about His intimate involvement in your life? What is your great-
    est takeaway from this passage?

PRACTICAL APPLICATION

But be doers of the word,
and not hearers only, deceiving yourselves.
— James 1:22

1. In this lesson, we learned that everything about you — your physical
    characteristics and mannerisms, the way you think, your personality,
    your weaknesses and strengths, even your life's experiences — all make
    you unique and enable you to fulfill God's assignment for your life.
    What is it about yourself that you have struggled to accept or even
    disliked? How is this lesson helping you see your qualities as positive
    rather than negative?

2. God called you to be *you* — not your best friend, your pastor, or one
    of your siblings. It is your job to learn what your calling is and cooper-
    ate with God to be the best "you" that you can be. Do you know what
    God has called you to do? If so, what is it? What has He specifically
    wired you and created you to accomplish, and are you doing it?

TOPIC

There Is Something You Must Hear

SCRIPTURES

1. **James 1:19** — So then, my beloved brethren, let every man be swift to hear, slow to speak, slow to wrath.
2. **Revelation 12:11** — And they overcame him by the blood of the Lamb and by the word of their testimony, and they did not love their lives to the death.

SYNOPSIS

In Lesson 1, we learned that God, of His own will, brought us forth by the word of truth (*see* James 1:18). Although your parents played an important part in birthing you on the earth, it was God who gave life to the specific egg and sperm that came together to form you. You are not the result of evolutionary chance — you are the result of His divine will. He chose you, and He quipped you to be the best you that you can be. To successfully carry out your calling, you need to hear — and keep hearing — the life-giving truth of God's Word.

The emphasis of this lesson:

In this broken world, where we face many difficulties and troubles, we need a steady intake of God's unchanging Word. We must choose to tune out the negative, doubtful, and fearful voices around us and tune in to the voice of the Holy Spirit speaking through the Scriptures.

The Way We Respond
in Times of Trouble Is Very Important

The book of James was written by James, the half-brother of Jesus. He was a major leader in the Early Church after Jesus' ascension back into Heaven and eventually took on the role of the pastor of the church in Jerusalem. With deep concern for his fellow believers, who were experiencing persecution and had been scattered across the Roman Empire, he wrote a letter to encourage them and teach them how to live.

He explained how God, of His own will, chose to create us and bring us forth in Christ. He then went on to say:

> **So then, my beloved brethren, let every man be swift to hear, slow to speak, slow to wrath.**
>
> **— James 1:19**

This powerful advice is just as important today as it was 2,000 years ago when it was first given. The way we respond to our troubles and trials will often determine how long they hang around. Let's face it, when we are going through times of temptation and suffering, our flesh is usually *quick to speak, quick to get angry*, and *slow to hear*. Responding in this way only serves to delay God's promises from being fulfilled in our lives.

We live in a fallen, broken world, and as human beings we have the ability to hurt one another very deeply. Likewise, our bodies can get sick, our marriages and families can become divided, our finances can shrivel, and our churches and communities can face turmoil. In such situations, it's crucial that we not accept every thought that drops into our head or listen to all the negative naysayers and news reports. Instead, we need to feed on the truth of God's Word and put our trust in Him.

What Are You Listening To?

One of the most unwise things you can do when you are trudging through challenges is listen to and believe what unbelievers are spouting off about you, about your situation, and about God. They just don't have the capacity to understand it. The apostle Paul made this clear in his first letter to the believers in Corinth, writing:

> **But the natural, nonspiritual man does not accept or welcome or admit into his heart the gifts and teachings and revelations of the Spirit of God, for they are folly (meaningless nonsense) to him; and he is incapable of knowing them [of progressively recognizing, understanding, and becoming better acquainted with them] because they are spiritually discerned and estimated and appreciated.**
>
> **— 1 Corinthians 2:14 *AMPC***

When you try to explain to an unbeliever what you're trusting God to do, they may mock and sneer at you, saying things like, "Why in the world are you believing that? It just doesn't make any sense. That's never going to happen. You're speaking false hope to yourself and setting yourself up for major disappointment."

Although opinions like these can come from well-meaning people who love you, their words are not God's Word. Only He can see all things at all times, and only He has all the answers. Thus, in those trying moments, it is imperative that you become swift to hear the Word of God and to listen to what the Holy Spirit is speaking — including what He is saying about how God made you.

Don't Listen to the Devil's Lies

Of course, recognizing and rejecting the enemy's voice is also a must in order for you to live in victory. He is the father of lies and there is no truth in him (*see* John 8:44). Swallowing his deceptions can definitely delay and detour you from God's plans. Denise shared about a time when she listened to the enemy and did something her parents told her not to do, and the side effects were long-lasting:

> Many years ago, when I was about ten years old, my parents went on a trip. While they were gone, my sister, my brother, and I stayed home and disobeyed my parents by watching a horror movie we were told not to watch. There was a strong spirit of fear attached to the movie, and it attached itself to me. That spirit of fear affected my life for several years.
>
> Again and again, fear lied to me and whispered thoughts like, *Somebody's going to get you,* and *You are going to die.* Those thoughts were accompanied by mental pictures and movies that constantly played on the screen of my mind, so much so that I began to believe they were true.
>
> There were even times when fear became so paralyzing, I was afraid to stay anywhere by myself. Fear had lodged itself in my heart and mind to the point that my imagination was out of control. It wasn't until I learned about the perfect love of God and understood that it casts out all fear that the spirit of fear was evicted from my life (*see* 1 John 4:18).

Thankfully, by learning the Word of God and listening to the wisdom of the Holy Spirit, I began to pull down the stronghold of fear and receive deliverance. Little by little, day by day, I sought the Lord, and He heard me, and delivered me from all my fears (*see* Psalm 34:4). Today I am free from that spirit of fear and all the lies that came with it.

If you are born again and fear is coming against you, it's time you stir up and awaken your spirit man and receive the empowerment of the Holy Spirit living in you. When you hear the enemy's lies, let your spirit man rise up on the inside of you and say, "No! That's not true, and I will not believe or give into fear. God has not given me a spirit of fear but a spirit of power, love, and a sound mind!" (*See* 2 Timothy 1:7.)

Friend, the devil is *not* omnipresent nor omnipotent — only God is. With God's strength, you can learn to become swift to hear, slow to speak, and slow to get angry. You can embrace and nurture your faith in God's Word and continue to hang on to it with every breath you take. These are the qualities needed to help see God's promises come to pass in your life and to become unstoppable.

Heather Z Was in a Fight for Her Life

Heather Z spoke about a life-threatening ordeal she experienced in which she had to learn to be quick to listen to God's Word, slow to speak, and slow to become angry. Here is what she shared:

At the age of 32, I was diagnosed with double kidney failure, which I learned was a hereditary disease. Day after day, the doctors told me I was going to die and that I needed to tell my husband and kids goodbye. It was extremely scary, as you can quite imagine.

The only option I had was to go on dialysis, which I did, and it became like a part-time job. Every other day, three to four days a week, I was hooked up to a machine for three to four hours, and that machine would filter all the impurities and excess fluid out of my body because my kidneys weren't functioning.

In the natural, everything I was seeing was very depressing. My body was frail, and my enzyme levels were all out of whack. The atmosphere of the dialysis unit itself was one of fear and hopelessness. I watched grown men stand by the doors and just break down and cry because there was no hope of them escaping death. Once a person started on dialysis, there was no guarantee of ever getting off. Most people stayed in treatment until it took their life or they were blessed to receive a kidney transplant.

During the two and a half years I was on dialysis, I formed relationships with the people receiving treatment with me. We usually showed up at the same time on the same days. But there were days I came in and the person that normally sat next to me was no longer there. Whenever there were flowers at the nurses' station, that was not a good day because it usually meant that someone had died, and the family members had brought flowers to thank the nurses for taking care of their loved ones.

So nothing about having kidney failure was good. If you didn't have the hope of Jesus and a revelation of His love and all He provided through the Cross, you were hopeless. In Christ, there is hope, healing, wholeness, and peace. Although most of us want to receive an instantaneous miracle from Jesus, often He gives us His healing in the form of a process that takes time. Through healing, we come to know and attain what is ours through Christ little by little.

Be Swift To Hear God's Word

To make it through the fight for her life, Heather had to **turn off certain things** and **turn on certain things**. She explained:

One thing I had to do was be very careful about who I was around. I had to stay away from or severely limit the time I spent with negative people. I was literally in a fight for my life and a fight for what I believed in and what I allowed into my mind.

All day, every day, I did nothing but read God's Word as much as I could, and I often read it aloud. When I couldn't physically read, I would listen to the Word on audio until it began to change my mind and my heart. I didn't know it at the time, but when I spoke God's Word out of my mouth and heard it, it would go into my ears and into my heart and build my faith.

Eventually, I began to have very tough days, and on one of those days, the Lord spoke to me and said, 'Heather, you have My power. I have breathed My power inside you.' That really encouraged me. Then He said, 'I want you to look at your hands and speak to them, telling them what you have through Me. Just as I spoke and created the world with My words, I want you to speak to your hands and release My creative power.'

So I began to speak to my hands and say things like, 'I have healing. The healing power of God is in my hands. I have wholeness in these hands. I have peace in these hands. I have all that Jesus provided through His death, burial, and resurrection in these hands.'

Then God told me to begin laying hands on myself, declaring that I had all these things that Jesus provided. As I did, I felt the presence and power of God in an amazing way. This practice encouraged my heart and brought me peace. I then began to speak peace over myself — peace over my mind, my emotions, and my heart. I also spoke and released peace into my physical body. By the way, the word 'peace' means *nothing broken and nothing lacking*. Everything Jesus provided through salvation, I spoke over my life and allowed myself to receive.

Everything We Do Is by Faith

Someone may look at his or her hands and say, "I can't see peace in my hands, nor can I see wholeness or healing. This must be some kind of psychological method of convincing oneself of something." That is not the case. Heather did all that she did *by faith*, and it is the same thing you must do to experience the promises of God that are available through Jesus.

We need to be swift to hear God's Word.

The Bible says, "Death and life are in the power of the tongue, and those who love it will eat its fruit" (Proverbs 18:21). By faith in this verse from God's Word, you can choose to use your mouth to *speak life* to your hands, your body, your relationships, and anything else that needs to be touched by God's power. That's what Heather did, and that is what you can do too!

The Bible also says that God's power is released through the laying on of hands (*see* 2 Timothy 1:6). Jesus Himself said, "And these signs will follow those who believe: In My name they will…lay hands on the sick, and they will recover" (Mark 16:17,18). By faith in verses like these from God's Word, you can take your hands and place them on yourself and on others and see recovery from all kinds of sicknesses and ailments. That's what Heather did, and that is what you can do too!

Faith always requires us to take action.

Heather shared how the Lord spoke to her heart and said, "There will be times when no one else is available to lay hands on you and pray for you. So I need to work through *you* to release My power." Acting in faith, Heather obeyed God's instructions, and He worked through her. He used the power of His Holy Spirit, which He had already placed inside her the moment she was saved.

Aligning ourselves with God's Word paves the way for His promises to become a reality.

To align yourself with God's Word is to get into agreement with Him, saying the same things He says. Because you are a believer, the Word is already in your spirit because the Spirit of Christ is living inside you — and *He* is the Word (*see* John 1:1).

Heather aligned herself with the Word that was inside her by looking at her hands and speaking God's Word to them with her mouth. Going further, she began placing her hands on her body, releasing God's power through her words and hands. That is the power of agreement. But it can only happen when we step out and operate by faith.

Faith is a gift given to us by God.

The moment you said *yes* to Jesus and received His salvation, the Holy Spirit took up permanent residence in you (*see* Galatians 4:6), and with Him came all the fruit of the Spirit (*see* Galatians 5:22,23). Even the faith needed to accept and serve Jesus was given to you by God (*see* Ephesians 2:8).

You activate your faith through the words you speak, through your cooperation with the Holy Spirit, and through your acts of obedience that lead to healing, wholeness, and peace. Every time you step out and act in faith, your faith grows, fear is pushed back, and you become unstoppable.

Heather's decision to continue to act in faith while battling double kidney failure is what opened the door to God's healing and restoration.

Get Into Agreement With God

Are you in need of God's healing touch or provisions? Well, you have God-breathed life on the inside of you, and that life is in your hands and in your mouth. You are a courier and carrier of the Holy Spirit and of salvation, which provides healing and wholeness. To be whole means to be fully restored back to the original state that God intended for your life, so by faith, declare that you have God's peace, power, healing, and life in your hands.

You can even lay hands on yourself and allow yourself to feel the power and presence of God working on the inside. God's power is working in your body, your mind, your heart, and your emotions. His power is resisting all fear and sickness and all doubt and unbelief. And He is providing healing and wholeness.

STUDY QUESTIONS

> Be diligent to present yourself approved to God,
> a worker who does not need to be ashamed,
> rightly dividing the word of truth.
> — 2 Timothy 2:15

1. Although everything around us is constantly changing, God's Word remains the same. It is the Book of all books, providing us with supernatural power, practical solutions, and timeless wisdom that transcends all trends. Take time to read Psalm 119:9; John 17:17; Romans 1:16; Ephesians 5:26; Second Timothy 3:16 and 17; Hebrews 4:12; and James 1:21 and identify the blessings you can expect as you make time to feed on God's Word.

2. Have you ever tried to explain something spiritual to an unbeliever, who just couldn't seem to grasp what you were saying? How does First Corinthians 2:14 (*AMPC*) help you better understand this type of situation? How might you pray in agreement with God's Word for that person to see and understand the truth (*see* 2 Corinthians 4:3-6)?

PRACTICAL APPLICATION

But be doers of the word,
and not hearers only, deceiving yourselves.
—James 1:22

1. Matthew 4:24 (*AMPC*) says, "…Be careful what you are hearing. The measure [of thought and study] you give [to the truth you hear] will be the measure [of virtue and knowledge] that comes back to you — and more [besides] will be given to you *who hear*." Examine the things you are hearing on a regular basis. Do those things line up with the truth of God's Word? Do they edify you and strengthen your faith? Or is what you are hearing bringing doubt, fear, and worry?

2. Every believer is in a spiritual fight for his or her life — against the enemy, the flesh, and against the world's system. Knowing God's Word is the greatest spiritual weapon you have. What can you do to get more of God's Word in you? Pray and ask the Holy Spirit to show you what you can eliminate from your life so you can spend more quality time in the Scriptures.

LESSON 3

TOPIC

Your Words Are Powerful

SCRIPTURES

1. **James 1:19** — So then, my beloved brethren, let every man be swift to hear, slow to speak, slow to wrath.

2. **Proverbs 15:28** — The heart of the righteous studies how to answer, but the mouth of the wicked pours forth evil.

3. **2 Corinthians 5:21** — For He made Him who knew no sin to be sin for us, that we might become the righteousness of God in Him.

4. **Proverbs 16:23** — The heart of the wise teaches his mouth, and adds learning to his lips.

5. **Proverbs 15:1** — A soft answer turns away wrath, but a harsh word stirs up anger.

SYNOPSIS

In the time in which we are living, there are many things pressing against us to try and stop us from moving forward in our race with Jesus. But the Author and Finisher of our faith has promised to stay with us through every step of our faith journey and take us all the way to the finish line!

Because you are a believer, the fullness of God's power resides in you, and as you put yourself in agreement with His Word — thinking it, speaking it, and acting on it — your life will continue to be transformed from the inside out. Even when you are faced with fiery confrontation, the Holy Spirit will teach you how to respond.

The emphasis of this lesson:

Along with guarding your ears, you must also guard your *mouth*. When problems pummel you, don't rehearse your pain and talk about how bad everything is. *Teach* your mouth how to respond. Draw from the strength of the Holy Spirit living in you and speak the promises of God's Word over your life and against the enemy.

A Review of Lessons 1 and 2

So far, we have learned that it was by God's will, not ours, that we were born again by the incorruptible Word of truth, which is Jesus (*see* 1 Peter 1:23). We didn't choose Him — He chose us, appointed us, and equipped us to live and bear abundant fruit (*see* John 15:16). In fact, the Bible says, "By his divine power, God has given us everything we need for living a godly life…" (2 Peter 1:3 *NLT*). It is all inside us.

God has fashioned and uniquely gifted each of us to carry out His specific assignments. No two of us are the same. Our physical characteristics, our mannerisms, the way we think and express ourselves, and even our experiences are all part of God's design and are needed to help us fulfill our purpose.

We also discovered that God wants us to be "…swift to hear, slow to speak, [and] slow to wrath" (James 1:19). It is so important that we learn to slow down our pace of life so that we can hear and receive the wisdom of the Lord. Any time we need help, we can pray and ask Him for understanding about what to do. But once we ask for His wisdom, we need to quiet our soul and get into a place where we can listen and hear what the Lord is saying and then respond in obedience.

The fullest life can only be lived by hearing and acting on the wisdom of the Lord.

When we are facing trials and troubles, we must tune in and hear what God's Word and His Spirit are saying and turn off what the negative naysayers are saying. Tuning in to people's opinions can be detrimental to our spiritual and physical health, as we saw in Heather Z's situation when she was in the fight for her life battling double kidney failure.

Many times, people came to her, saying things that seemed to be filled with concern but were actually fearful, "what-if" scenarios that she could not afford to entertain. Even though these concerns were real, and the potential negative outcomes were common for others in similar situations, she had to choose to not listen to them. Her life depended on her taking in the truth of God's Word and shutting out negative, fearful reports. The same holds true for you — especially when you are in a fight for your life.

A major key to gaining and maintaining a sound, sane mind and a heart of faith is learning to live fully saturated in God's Word. As you continue to hear and hear and hear God's Word — reading, studying, meditating, and listening to God's Word — your soul and spirit will reach a level of saturation where God's thoughts become your thoughts, and His Word becomes the governing force in your life, molding and shaping your every decision.

To be clear, when you are on the battlefield in the fight for your life, you don't need to be listening to people telling you how bad the battle is. Their doubts and fears will only serve to distract, derail, and drain you of strength. What you need most is to be saturated in the Word of God and filled with the Holy Spirit. That is your "battle-ready" equipment. The Spirit brings amazing heart-revelation of God's Word and provides the divine empowerment you need to make it through any crisis you're facing.

There Is a Time When You Need To 'Go Sterile'

Heather shared how she and her husband Joseph both studied and trained to become pilots. During that training, they learned that there is a certain time during a flight that is called the "sterile zone," which is when an aircraft starts to ascend at takeoff and when it starts to descend at landing. In the same way an operating room is sterile and void of contamination, the sterile zone during flight is void of conversation. When those in the cockpit "go sterile," there is absolutely no talking between the pilot and copilot.

It's in those eight minutes going up and eight minutes coming down that the pilot and copilot must be fully listening and fully engaged with their eyes and ears, paying attention to every instrument in front of them. It has been said that those who break the rules and start talking during the sterile zone experience a high percentage of crashes and often don't make it out alive.

Spiritually speaking, there is a "sterile zone" that we as believers must go through during trials and troubles. These are times or seasons when it is vital that we remain quiet and shut out the voices of those around us. Our undivided focus needs to be on the "instruments" in front of us, which would include God's Word, the leadership of the Holy Spirit, and the God-honoring people He has placed in our lives. We need to be aware of them and work with them because our life may depend on it.

Desperate times call for desperate measures. When your world seems to be falling apart and the enemy is bombarding your brain with thoughts and imaginations of doom and gloom, you need to guard your ears — taking hold of what God has promised in His Word and what He has spoken to your heart by His Spirit.

Watch Your Words

In addition to guarding your ears, you also need to guard your mouth. What you say can and will be used against you by the enemy. Again, "Death and life are in the power of the tongue…" (Proverbs 18:21). That includes *your* tongue. The words you speak will either be life-giving or death-inducing.

While battling double kidney failure, there were countless times when Heather experienced a great deal of physical pain, discouraging setbacks, and frustrating challenges. In those very real and quite overwhelming moments, she felt like saying things to voice the mental and emotional pain she was feeling. But knowing that her life would be greatly impacted by what she said, she remained silent.

Our first response when trouble and tragedy strike is most crucial to the outcome.

When you receive bad news about anything, your first response to that information is the most important. Life and death are in the power of your tongue, so the first words out of your mouth are vital and can literally save your life.

Consider blind Bartimaeus. His first response when he heard that Jesus of Nazareth was coming was to cry out to Him. He didn't cry out to his neighbors, his friends, or government officials. He opened his mouth and called out directly to Jesus, saying, "...Jesus, Son of David, have mercy on me!" (Mark 10:47). Bartimaeus' desperate plea reached the ears of Jesus, causing Him to stop, stand still, and call Bartimaeus to Him. This demonstrates how there is a direct line from our spirit to God's Spirit.

Friend, when problems pummel you, don't rehearse your pain and talk about how bad everything is. If you feel the urge to say things like, "This will never work out. Things have been this way for years, and they're never going to change," ask God for the strength not to say it. Instead, use your mouth as a weapon against the enemy. Speak the promises of God's Word against sickness, financial lack, doubt and fear, and anything else that comes against you.

Study How To Answer

Being "slow to speak" means we need to think about what we're going to say *before* we say it. Before words just start flying out of our mouth, we need to calculate what our words are going to produce. When God and Jesus spoke, their words released creative power that formed and changed the world. We are made in God's image, and that same creative power lives on the inside of us.

Regarding God's words, the psalmist said, "Your word is a lamp to my feet and a light to my path" (Psalm 119:105). Similarly, our words are a lamp for where we are presently and a light for the road to our future. What we say creates a pathway on which we walk. Again, this tells us we need to think before we speak — and *carefully* choose our words.

Scripture backs this up, telling us:

> **The heart of the righteous studies how to answer, but the mouth of the wicked pours forth evil.**
>
> **— Proverbs 15:28**

Imagine for a moment that you are in a difficult situation where your words could really get you into trouble. You're talking with someone and can feel the heat of anger starting to rise out of your soul. Your patience has worn thin with this person because they are once again acting in a way that sets you off. In the heat of that moment, you've got to *study how to answer.*

In practical terms, one of the best things you can do in such a situation is say to the person, "Would you excuse me for a few minutes? I really don't know what to say right now." Then take yourself out of the situation. Go into another room, the restroom, or simply step outside. Count to 10 — or 100 if needed — and pray. Sometimes the only words you can muster are, "Help me, Jesus!" And that is a perfect prayer of humility that acknowledges your desperate need for the Lord's help.

It's all about self-control, which is one of the fruits of the Spirit that is already in you because the Holy Spirit is living in you. It just needs to be developed through use. You can actually become very intentional about how you respond by developing self-control.

Silence Is Golden

There's an old saying you may have heard: "If you don't have anything nice to say, don't say anything at all." This is still great wisdom that will save you from much heartache if you follow it. Right now, you may be on a journey with a close friend, a relative, or maybe even your spouse, working through some recurring challenges. The fact is, you both need grace and space to grow. So give those people — *and yourself* — grace and space in the areas where growth is needed.

Extending grace and space for others sometimes looks like *silence* on your part. Remember, there is a time for everything under the sun, including "…a time to keep silence…" (Ecclesiastes 3:7). So if you don't have anything nice to say — *even about yourself* — remain silent. Give the Holy Spirit time to heal your heart and mind.

It's perfectly acceptable to "press pause" on life and just *breathe*. Silence is golden; it provides a window of opportunity to study how to answer others. The Bible says, "Even fools are thought wise if they keep silent, and discerning if they hold their tongues" (Proverbs 17:28 *NIV*).

The Word of God is a treasure chest that contains everything you need — including the wisdom required to know what to say in a heated situation. So continue to search the Scriptures for the answers you need.

The Heart of the Wise
Teaches His Mouth To Respond

Another wonderful scripture regarding the mouth and learning to respond correctly is Proverbs 16:23, which says, "The heart of the wise teaches his mouth, and adds learning to his lips." If you have a desire to answer in a right, godly way, then you have the heart of the wise, and you teach your mouth what it's going to say. The teacher is not your emotions or your circumstances; the teacher of your mouth is your spirit man.

Notice this verse doesn't say, "The wise teaches his mouth...." It says, "The *heart* of the wise teaches his mouth..." (Proverbs 16:23). If it just said, "The wise teaches his mouth," it would leave room for pride to develop. The fact that the Bible says, "The *heart* of the wise teaches his mouth" means you have the heart to be wise and you're able to teach your mouth because your heart is humble and teachable.

This verse also reveals that it is our responsibility to teach our mouth. We can't hide behind excuses like, "Well, my mother and my grandmother used to scream and cuss at me all the time. And my father was an alcoholic whose words were often out of control. I just don't know how to respond correctly." That is not true, because you have the Holy Spirit living on the inside of you, and you have the heart of the wise. And since you have the heart of the wise, *your heart* is the teacher. It's not your parents, your past, your spouse, or your situation. You are the teacher, and therefore, you have the divine power to experience the best outcome you could possibly have.

Proverbs 15:1 also talks about the mouth, saying, "A soft answer turns away wrath, but a harsh word stirs up anger." The phrase "turns away" could also be translated as *rebukes*. Thus, a soft answer — a gentle, peaceable response — rebukes wrath. You want peace wrapped around your words, because it is peaceful words that pack the power to rebuke and stop wrath. When you choose to allow your heart to teach your mouth what to say and not let your emotions, your past, or your situation teach you how to respond, you will speak words of peace regardless of how volatile the other person responds.

The next time you find yourself in a situation where your mouth is about to get you into trouble, take a moment to open your heart up to the Lord and say, "I'm here and I'm ready to receive your wisdom and strength. I'm setting aside the offense, the pain, and my emotions, which feel very real right now, and I'm leaving room to listen to You. You are my Teacher, Holy Spirit. Lead me and teach me how to conduct myself. In Jesus' name. Amen."

STUDY QUESTIONS

> Be diligent to present yourself approved to God,
> a worker who does not need to be ashamed,
> rightly dividing the word of truth.
> — 2 Timothy 2:15

The Bible has much to say about the mouth — things you really need to know. Take time to look up these verses and identify what God says about the importance and power of your words.

- Why is it valuable to carefully choose our words?
  (*See* Proverbs 10:19; 13:3; 21:23.)

- How does the Bible define *good* words?
  (*See* Proverbs 16:24; Ephesians 4:29; Colossians 4:6)

- What did David ask God to do with his mouth that you can ask for too? (*See* Psalm 141:3.)

PRACTICAL APPLICATION

> But be doers of the word,
> and not hearers only, deceiving yourselves.
> — James 1:22

1. What would you say is your typical first response when you receive bad news about something? How is this lesson causing you to rethink how you respond?

2. If you have ever wondered how powerful your words are in God's eyes, wonder no longer. Read James 3:1-12 and listen for what the Holy Spirit says to you about the power of your tongue.

TOPIC

Bitterness Never Looks Good on You

SCRIPTURES

1. **James 1:18,19** — Of His own will He brought us forth by the word of truth, that we might be a kind of firstfruits of His creatures. So then, my beloved brethren, let every man be swift to hear, slow to speak, slow to wrath.
2. **Proverbs 15:1** — A soft answer turns away wrath, but a harsh word stirs up anger.
3. **Proverbs 16:32** — He who is slow to anger is better than the mighty, and he who rules his spirit than he who takes a city.

SYNOPSIS

Knowing who you are called to be starts with knowing you were purposely picked by God to be in relationship with Him. James 1:18 says, "*Of His own will* He brought us forth by the word of truth…." When you look at this verse in some commentaries, it depicts God sitting down and counseling with Himself and basically telling Himself, "This is My will: I'm going to choose that person [*YOU!*]."

What a miracle! You are not an accident. The God of all creation *intentionally* created you. Whether your parents planned your life or not, God planned it. He then came into your life on the day you were saved and gave you the faith to believe in and receive Jesus as your Lord and Savior. You are chosen! You have a purpose, and you are deeply loved by your Heavenly Father!

The emphasis of this lesson:

Opportunities to be offended and get upset are never ending. But God has given us the power of His Holy Spirit to deal with anger before it becomes deep-seated. When we practice self-control and are slow to anger, we are stronger in God's eyes than a warrior who conquers a city.

You Are Accepted — Not Rejected

There is a true story about a woman preacher who, when she was 35 years old, discovered a family secret that had been hidden from her for more than three decades. One morning, when she was spending time in her mother's house, she inadvertently ran across documents revealing that the woman she called Mom wasn't her birth mother. Her biological mother had put her up for adoption shortly after she was born.

Incredibly dazed by the discovery, this young woman had an immediate desire to seek and find her birth mother, which is exactly what she did. The day eventually came when she journeyed to her biological mother's house. By that time, this beautiful, 35-year-old preacher had been quite successful in ministry, and she couldn't wait to meet the woman who had given birth to her and tell her how greatly God was using her.

Bursting with excitement, she walked up to the door, knocked, and waited with great anticipation. With the sliding sound of the deadbolt and the turning of the knob, the door opened, and the young woman presented herself.

"Hello! I am your daughter," she said with a voice full of hopeful expectation. "And you're my Mom!"

With great shock, her birth mother looked at her and said, "I don't want any part of you. I didn't want you then, and I don't want you now." And with that, she shut the door in the young woman's face.

Can you imagine how rejected she must have felt? She thought, *What do I do with this?* In that moment, that young woman had a choice to make: allow rejection to take root in her soul or look deeper into what God had done for her.

Suddenly, the Holy Spirit brought to her remembrance a powerful verse of Scripture found in Ephesians 1:4, which declares:

...He chose us in Him before the foundation of the world, that we should be holy and without blame before Him in love.

Holding tightly to that powerful promise, the young woman said to herself as if she was talking to her Mom, *You didn't choose me, but God did.*

Maybe you can identify with the level of rejection this young woman experienced. If so, God wants you to know that no matter how much rejection has been dealt to you, **He chose you as an act of His will**, and the Bible says, "…He made us accepted in the Beloved" (Ephesians 1:6). He brought you forth by the word of truth, and your life has great purpose in Him!

Deal With Anger Before It Becomes 'Deep Seated'

Looking once more at our anchor verse, it says, "So then, my beloved brethren, let every man be swift to hear, slow to speak, slow to wrath" (James 1:19).

Notice the words *slow to wrath*. When you study this phrase out in the original Greek, you find that it would be better translated *slow to deep-seated wrath*. The fact that this wrath is "deep-seated" indicates it developed over time, not overnight. Therefore, since it is a process, we can make a decision to deal with the hurt and address the offense so that it doesn't become deep-seated.

You have the power to stop and recognize the situation and take yourself out of it, which is what we covered in Lesson 3. When you are on the brink of a blowup, simply say to the person, "Would you excuse me for a few minutes? I really don't know what to say right now." Then take yourself out of the situation. Go into another room and count to 10 — or to 100 if needed — and pray.

This window of time enables you to invite the supernatural power of the Holy Spirit into the situation and begin exercising self-control, which is a fruit of the Spirit. The alternative — screaming at each other and tearing one another apart with your words — is costly and gets you nowhere. In such a state, no one is in control, and there is total confusion. Taking the time to step out and remove yourself allows you to regain peace and be in a position to offer a peaceful answer just as Proverbs 15:1 instructs us:

A soft answer turns away wrath, but a harsh word stirs up anger.

Again, when you give a peaceful, gentle answer, it rebukes wrath. That is what happened when Jesus and His disciples were in their boat and a storm came against them. According to Mark 4:37 (*AMPC*), it was "…a furious storm of wind [of hurricane proportions]…." The original Greek text reveals that the waves were being picked up by a supernatural force and thrown against the ship. Thus, this was not an ordinary storm. But when Jesus stood up and spoke the word *peace* to the storm, the wrath was turned away! This is a picture of Jesus teaching His mouth what to say. Rather than allow the situation or people's emotions dictate His response, Jesus employed peace to do the job of rebuking the wrath of the storm — and He was successful.

Exercising Self-Control Makes You Mighty in God's Eyes

James is not the only writer to teach us about being slow to wrath. King Solomon offers very similar instructions in Proverbs 16:32, which says:

He who is slow to anger is better than the mighty, and he who rules his spirit than he who takes a city.

There have been many great leaders throughout history who are renowned for their military successes. Stories have been written and statues have been erected in their honor. This includes generals like George Washington who led the colonies to victory over Great Britain; George Patton who won multiple battles in World War II; and Alexander the Great who conquered the known world in the Fourth Century. Indeed, these men and others are certainly highly respected giants on the battlefield.

Yet in God's eyes, when we are slow to anger, we are better than these mighty men. And when we practice self-control and rule our own spirit, we are mightier than those who take a city. That is powerful!

Right now, you may be dealing with anger over what your spouse, a family member, a coworker, or someone else has done to you. The offense did happen, and the hurt is real. But thank God, through the power of the Holy Spirit, you can begin to seek Him for the healing you need. Simply come to Him, and as an act of your will, set your emotions aside and get real with Him. Say, "Lord, I'm really upset right now, but I am coming to You for the strength I need to *not* keep responding in anger the way my flesh wants to. Help me, Lord. In Jesus' name."

That is what it looks like to become strong and mighty in God's eyes. The Lord will give you the power to "press pause" on the troubling events you've experienced so they no longer rule your life.

Give Yourself a Good Talking-To

When you refuse to get into an argument or you walk away from it, you are a warrior in God's eyes. Likewise, when you speak to your soul and say, "Calm down, emotions; be at peace, mind," in God's opinion, you are more powerful than a four-star general who conquers a city.

Like David, sometimes you just need to give yourself a good talking-to! Again and again throughout the Psalms, David pulled away on his own and said to himself things like, "Why are you cast down, O my soul? And why are you disquieted within me? Hope in God; for I shall yet praise Him..." (Psalm 42:11).

When you step away from an escalating situation and give yourself some healthy self-talk, you slow things down and disrupt the pattern of rising frustration and irritation in your soul. The chemical endorphins that were preparing you for fight or flight will begin to diminish, and the explosion that was about to happen will be diffused. These are all steps to you gaining power and control of your own life, as well as putting a stop to any potential damage you could have caused to someone else.

The truth is, when we abandon all restraint and allow ourselves to cut loose in a fit of rage, it is absolutely exhausting. If you have ever lost control and given yourself to an angry "flesh fit," you know how terrible you feel afterwards. In addition to feeling bad physically, the Holy Spirit living in your spirit is grieved and grows quiet. Paul cautions us against this in Ephesians 4:30.

Thankfully, we don't have to go there. When things are getting out of control, we can learn to pull ourselves aside and talk to ourselves and say something like, "You know what, I don't like your attitude right now, so chill out. Take a minute to breathe and calm down." That's what it looks like for you to agree with the power of the Holy Spirit on the inside of you. It is a picture of being slow to anger and exercising self-control. That's you taking control of your own life and actions and at the same time, protecting others from potential pain.

The Humble Get God's Help

Realize the only thing that would cause us to stay in an argument is pride, and the Bible says that God *resists* the proud (*see* James 4:6). The word "resist" here means *to stand against like an army*, which is exactly what God does when we operate in pride. In contrast, He gives grace to the humble. So when we step away from a situation to pray and take control of our mind and emotions, we are humbling ourselves, which invites the grace and power of the Holy Spirit that is on the inside of us to strengthen us to walk in self-control.

It may be that you are reading this right now, and you are going through a very difficult situation. Maybe you have an alcoholic spouse, or you are dealing with a drug-addicted child who screams and curses at you, and you don't know what to do. Thank God, His mighty Spirit is living inside you, providing you with the fruit of self-control. If you will humble yourself and ask Him for help, He will give you the grace to control yourself. And in His eyes, that makes you mightier than one who takes a city (*see* Proverbs 16:32). That's how much power God invested in you the moment you were born again.

Friend, you are not alone. The Holy Spirit is always with you, and you can talk to Him anytime, anywhere, about anything. This is your journey of studying and learning how to walk in self-control so that you are no longer ruled by your emotions. As you continue to humble yourself and learn to rule your spirit, you become the general of your life as well as a general in the lives of your family, friends, and coworkers. The more you become a person of self-control, the more your level of influence will grow.

Why is it so important that we are quick to hear, slow to speak, and slow to anger? James 1:20 tells us, "For the wrath of man does not produce the righteousness of God." In other words, getting angry, exploding, and unloading on others does not produce or cultivate good character. Only godly character in us — a soft answer, self-control, and patience — will produce godly character in others.

STUDY QUESTIONS

Be diligent to present yourself approved to God,
a worker who does not need to be ashamed,
rightly dividing the word of truth.
— 2 Timothy 2:15

1. Jesus said, "…It is impossible that no offenses should come…" (Luke 17:1). Since we cannot escape being hurt by others, we need to learn how to deal with our hurts in the right way. Take a careful

look at Ephesians 4:26 and 27 and Psalm 37:1-9 and write down the biblical steps to properly process our anger.

2. The apostle Paul cautioned us not to *grieve* the Holy Spirit when we are dealing with anger. Take time to reflect on Ephesians 4:25-32, paying close attention to verses 29-32. What actions cause the Holy Spirit to be grieved? What does God's Word say we need to do to avoid grieving the Spirit?

3. To deal with difficulties, "…[God] gives us more and more grace (power of the Holy Spirit, to meet this evil tendency and all others fully). That is why He says, God sets Himself against the proud and haughty, but gives grace [continually] to the lowly (those who are humble enough to receive it)" (James 4:6 *AMPC*). This truth is also found in First Peter 5:5 and Proverbs 3:34. What are the rewards of cultivating a heart of humility? Consider these verses:

    •   Psalm 25:9 and 147:6

    •   Proverbs 11:2; 15:33; 22:4; 29:23

    •   James 4:10 and 1 Peter 5:6

PRACTICAL APPLICATION

But be doers of the word,
and not hearers only, deceiving yourselves.
—James 1:22

1. Are you dealing with a situation that is hurtful and offensive — one that could potentially lead to *deep-seated* wrath? If so, briefly describe what you are walking through.

2. Now take your circumstances to the Lord and pour your heart out to Him in prayer (*see* Psalm 62:8). Invite the Holy Spirit into the situation, asking Him for His supernatural power to exercise self-control as He goes to work on your behalf. He loves you and has your best interest at heart. He also knows how to fix what seems unfixable and heal the hurts that we have experienced.

TOPIC

Don't Forget What You Saw in the Mirror

SCRIPTURES

1. **James 1:18** — Of His own will He brought us forth by the word of truth, that we might be a kind of firstfruits of His creatures.

2. **James 1:21-25**— Therefore lay aside all filthiness and overflow of wickedness, and receive with meekness the implanted word, which is able to save your souls. But be doers of the word, and not hearers only, deceiving yourselves. For if anyone is a hearer of the word and not a doer, he is like a man observing his natural face in a mirror; for he observes himself, goes away, and immediately forgets what kind of man he was. But he who looks into the perfect law of liberty and continues in it, and is not a forgetful hearer but a doer of the work, this one will be blessed in what he does.

3. **Romans 12:2** — And do not be conformed to this world, but be transformed by the renewing of your mind, that you may prove what is that good and acceptable and perfect will of God.

SYNOPSIS

If there was one step that you could take — and keep on taking — to see real victory and experience positive change in your life, that step would be to CONTINUE. The Bible says, "But he who looks into the perfect law of liberty and **continues** in it, and is not a forgetful hearer but a doer of the work, this one will be blessed in what he does" (James 1:25).

This final lesson packs the potential to change your life forever. It is all about *continuing* in the unchanging, supernatural power of God's Word. Nothing in this life — *nothing* — will have a greater impact on you than spending consistent time in Scripture.

The emphasis of this lesson:

Understanding who you are called to be is inseparably linked to your interaction with God's Word. He wants you to recognize and remove the unhealthy, ungodly things from your life and humbly receive His truth. Once you hear the Word, He calls you to *do* it. The transformation of your character will most certainly come as you continue in His truth.

A Quick Review

So far, we have studied James 1:18, which says, "Of His own will He brought us forth by the word of truth, that we might be a kind of firstfruits of His creatures." Therefore, you are not an accident; God birthed you for a purpose.

We also looked at James 1:19, which says, "…Let every man be swift to hear, slow to speak, slow to wrath." What we're to be swift to hear is the Word of God, which has all the answers we need and is unchanging truth. At the same time, we are to be slow to speak and slow to wrath or anger. We can do all three of these things through the power of the Holy Spirit who is living inside us. These are qualities we need in order to become mature believers and walk out God's divine purpose for our life.

Jesus said that it is impossible to avoid offenses (*see* Luke 17:1). So because they are going to come our way, we need to learn how to deal with offenses correctly. Thankfully, God has given us the power of His Holy Spirit to deal with anger before it becomes deep-seated. When we practice self-control and are slow to anger, we are stronger in God eyes than a warrior who conquers a city.

'Lay Aside All Filthiness
and the Overflow of Wickedness'

James 1:21 goes on to say, "Therefore lay aside all filthiness and overflow of wickedness, and receive with meekness the implanted word, which is able to save your souls." There are two actions we are instructed to do in this verse. First, we are to "lay aside all filthiness and overflow of wickedness," and second, we are to "receive God's Word."

What is interesting about the words "lay aside" is that they carry the idea of *taking something off oneself and pushing it so far out of reach that you cannot easily pick it up again.* This indicates that we need to personally take action and get involved. For example, at the end of each day, our clothes are not going to just fall off of us. We must purposely take hold of them and take them off. In this passage, we are specifically instructed to lay aside "all *filthiness* and the overflow of *wickedness.*"

Friend, if the Holy Spirit is asking you to lay something aside, it's because He has something better for you. There is a blessing of some kind just around the corner, and if you will be obedient and lay that thing aside, He will give you something greater. You are not going to be without what you need. Remember, the Lord is your Shepherd, and you will not lack or be in want (*see* Psalm 23:1).

One of the things the Holy Spirit is going to give you is revelation from God's Word that is so powerful it will *save your soul*. It will cause you to think right and act right. But you can only hear and receive this truth if you lay aside the things you know you need to let go of.

When you humble yourself and say, "Lord, I don't want to do this any-more, so I lay it aside. Please help me. By faith, I receive Your Word. In Jesus' name…," that is the kind of prayer that will enable your soul to be saved.

Be a 'Doer' of the Word

James, being the great pastor that he was, went on to elaborate on these instructions about laying aside and receiving. He said, "But be doers of the word, and not hearers only, deceiving yourselves" (James 1:22). This sobering verse tells us that if we only hear God's Word and don't *do* it, something really bad happens: we deceive ourselves, convincing ourselves.

When we deceive ourselves, it is much like a farmer who begins to think about planting seed in the ground, imagines reaping a bumper crop, but never actually plants any seed. He just reads and thinks about it. How do you think that is going to turn out for him? Will he actually reap a harvest by just reading and thinking about planting seed but never doing the work of putting seed into the ground? No.

Likewise, that is what happens when we merely think about God's Word but never put forth the effort to do it. When we hear the Word, and then tell ourselves things like, *I don't want to do that. I know I need to, but I just don't feel like it. God will understand*, that is very dangerous thinking because it opens us up to deception.

The truth is, in some of our most difficult moments, when we need to take action and no longer just talk about the Word, that is often the time we experience the greatest spiritual growth and receive the most revelation and understanding of truth. That growth and understanding then enables us to give back and pour into the lives of others.

An Example of a 'Doer'

Let's say that a husband and wife have a disagreement, and the Holy Spirit begins to nudge the wife to take the first step to restore unity. Of course, she wants her husband to apologize to her first, but the Holy Spirit keeps nudging *her* to take the first step and apologize. Perhaps her conversation with the Holy Spirit sounds something like this:

"Ask him to forgive you for being disrespectful," the Spirit says to her.

"Me, disrespectful?" She argues with the Lord. "Well, what about him and what he did!"

"I'm not talking about him right now," the Holy Spirit responds. "I'm talking about *you*. And even if you were right in this argument, the fact that you were disrespectful in how you handled yourself means you have room to apologize."

With a desire to honor and please the Lord, the wife humbles herself and says to her husband, "I'm sorry. I was disrespectful in the way I spoke to you. Please forgive me."

That kind of God-directed action ushers the Holy Spirit right into that argument. Like water on a fire, the wife's humble act of obedience releases the Spirit's power to extinguish the offense and restore peace.

The truth is, we can be right and yet still be wrong because of our attitude. But by responding with humility, even though it's difficult and doesn't feel good, it puts out the fire of conflict, and the outcome of humility and reconciliation is so much sweeter for everyone involved.

Friend, God is not asking us to feel good about doing the Word. He's just asking us to do it. And when we are obedient, we will be blessed.

An Example of a 'Hearer' Only

So what happens when we don't obey God's Word? James 1:22 and 23 tells us, "For if anyone is a hearer of the word and not a doer, he is like a man observing his natural face in a mirror; for he observes himself, goes away, and immediately forgets what kind of man he was." To help us understand what James is saying here, let's look again at our example of a husband and wife who have had a disagreement.

As before, the wife has looked into the "mirror" of God's Word and read passages that say wives are to be respectful and submissive to their husbands (*see* Ephesians 5:22-24). But once she puts down the "mirror" of the Word, she begins to listen to her own natural reasoning.

What about him? she says to herself. *What about what he said and how he acted?*

Immediately, she forgets what God said in His Word about her actions because she becomes so focused on what her husband did. Even worse, because she chose not to obey the Word, she is deceived about what *she* did, how *she* acted, and what *she* could have done better.

To be clear, the full power of God's Word in one's life is not in just the hearing of the Word — nor is it in the teaching of the Word. Although these are vital, the full power of God's Word is released in one's life through doing the Word.

God has called each of us to be a hands-on learner. Rather than just hear instruction, He wants us to *act out* His Word. It's very similar to how we go about learning a new skill. Many times, hearing someone lecture about it isn't enough. What we need is to actually do it ourselves.

So the next time you sense the Holy Spirit telling you to humble yourself and do something you don't *feel* like doing, go ahead and act it out. Your prompt obedience will make you a doer of the Word and begin to seal the truth in your heart. It will course-correct your character and serve to encourage and strengthen you for the next thing God asks you to do.

Continuing in the Word
Is Renewing Your Mind

James wraps up his teaching on being a doer of the Word by telling us, "But he who looks into the perfect law of liberty and continues in it, and is not a forgetful hearer but a doer of the work, this one will be blessed in what he does" (James 1:25). Please don't miss this very important truth:

Once you start looking into God's Word, you must *continue* looking into God's Word.

The power of continuing is probably best seen when we see something in the Word that we don't want to do, but we keep looking at it and remain open to doing it. For instance, let's say you struggle with Philippians 2:14 (*NLT*), which says, "Do everything without complaining and arguing." By *continuing in this verse* — looking at it with your eyes, meditating on it in your mind, and speaking it out of your mouth — your mind is being renewed, and God's thoughts are becoming your thoughts.

Romans 12:2 says, "And do not be conformed to this world, but be transformed by the renewing of your mind, that you may prove what is that good and acceptable and perfect will of God." Thus, **continuing in the Word is renewing your mind**, and the more you practice, practice, practice, the more you are becoming a person who knows the perfect will of God.

Continuing in the Word is all about putting time into being a doer of the Word, which is putting time into practicing the character of Christ until you begin — by HIS power — to master it. This means it is no longer painful or something hard to do. Instead, it is second nature.

Continuing in the Word
Brings Stability and Great Blessings

Eventually, the result of continuing in the Word will be *stability*, when you are no longer emotionally up one minute and down the next. Although you're not doing everything perfectly, you are no longer rocked every time something unpleasant or bad happens. Instead, you remain emotionally stable because you have a heart-revelation of the Word — practicing it becomes part of your everyday life. Instead of being moved by your emotions, you are moved by the Word of God.

In this condition, you are a healthier, happier person — a better worker, better friend, better spouse, better parent — a more peaceful person all around. That is what the Bible means when it says, "…this one will be blessed in what he does" (James 1:25).

Friend, if you live moved by your circumstances, your opinions, and the opinions of others, then you will live an out-of-control, rollercoaster life filled with emotional ups and downs. But when you choose to be a doer of the Word — *and continue in it* — the Word will keep coming and coming and coming into you, saving your soul (your mind, will, and emotions) just like the Scripture says. And you will be blessed in all you do! That is what it looks like to walk and live in victory.

If it's not happening inside you right now, don't be discouraged, just *continue in the Word*. It has indescribable power. The more you see the Word with your eyes, hear the Word with your ears, and speak the Word with your mouth, the more change it will bring to your life. It is healing to your flesh! (*See* Proverbs 4:20-22.)

STUDY QUESTIONS

**Be diligent to present yourself approved to God,
a worker who does not need to be ashamed,
rightly dividing the word of truth.
— 2 Timothy 2:15**

1. The Word of God is truly transformative! You can read countless books, but only one book reads you — *the Bible.* The improvements and continual upgrades that come with continuing in God's Word are incalculable! Read Psalm 119:9; Romans 1:16; and Second Timothy 3:16 and 17. What benefits does God's Word guarantee?
2. Read Philippians 2:12 and 13 (*AMPC*) and First Thessalonians 5:23 and 24 (*AMPC*). What is the Holy Spirit revealing to you in these verses? What is HIS part in the process of changing you?

PRACTICAL APPLICATION

**But be doers of the word,
and not hearers only, deceiving yourselves.
— James 1:22**

1. God's Word tells us to "…lay aside all filthiness and overflow of wickedness…" (James 1:21). Is there something (or someone) you're involved with that you know is not healthy for you and from which you need to distance yourself? What (or who) is it? What steps can you take right now to lay this aside — to take it off and push it so far out of reach that you cannot easily pick it up again?

2. Would you say you are a *doer* of the Word? How do you think your closest family members and friends would respond if asked this question about you? What about God? Would He say you're a doer of the Word or more of a *hearer*? What evidence in your life backs up these answers?

A Prayer To Receive Salvation

If you've never received Jesus as your Savior and Lord, now is the time for you to experience the new life Jesus wants to give you! To receive God's gift of salvation that can be obtained through Jesus alone, pray this prayer from your heart:

> *Jesus, I repent of my sin and receive You as my Savior and Lord. Wash away my sin with Your precious blood and make me completely new. I thank You that my sin is removed, and Satan no longer has any right to lay claim on me. Through Your empowering grace, I faithfully promise that I will serve You as my Lord for the rest of my life.*

If you just prayed this prayer of salvation, you are born again! You are a brand-new creation in Christ! Would you please let us know of your decision by going to **renner.org/salvation**? We would love to connect with you and pray for you as you begin your new life in Christ.

Scriptures for further study: John 3:16; John 14:6; Acts 4:12; Ephesians 1:7; Hebrews 10:19,20; 1 Peter 1:18,19; Romans 10:9,10; Colossians 1:13; 2 Corinthians 5:17; Romans 6:4; 1 Peter 1:3

Notes

Notes

CLAIM YOUR FREE RESOURCE!

As a way of introducing you further to the teaching ministry of Rick Renner, we would like to send you FREE of charge his teaching, "How To Receive a Miraculous Touch From God" on CD or USB format.

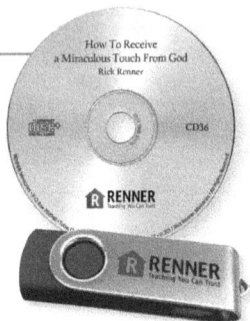

In His earthly ministry, Jesus commonly healed *all* who were sick of *all* their diseases. In this profound message, learn about the manifold dimensions of Christ's wisdom, goodness power, and love toward all humanity who came to Him in faith with their needs.

☑ **YES, I want to receive Rick Renner's monthly teaching letter!**

Simply scan the QR code to claim this resource or go to: **renner.org/claim-your-free-offer**

Connect WITH US!

R renner.org

facebook.com/rickrenner • facebook.com/rennerdenise

youtube.com/rennerministries • youtube.com/deniserenner

instagram.com/rickrenner • instagram.com/rennerministries_
instagram.com/rennerdenise

*9 7 8 1 6 6 7 5 0 9 6 4 8 *